The ABCs of Being a
Super Girl-Dad

written by Tyson Bell

Illustrator Chloé Elimam

Watersprings
PUBLISHING

The ABC'S of Being a Super Girl-Dad
published by Watersprings Publishing,
a division of Watersprings Media House, LLC.

P.O. Box 1284 Olive Branch, MS 38654

www.waterspringpublishing.com

Contact the publisher for bulk orders and permission requests.

Printed in the United States of America.

ISBN-13: 979-8-9894494-2-2

Always help bring out her inner <u>A</u>rtist while trying your best not to fall off the couch.

4

5

Bb

Be willing to dress up in more than just your superhero costume.

<u>C</u>arry your first-aid kit in your utility belt for occasional "boo-boos."

Dd

Dance, dance, dance, even though when you are done, your feet may be sore, sore, sore.

Ee

Eat anything she makes for you, no matter how weird it looks or tastes.

13

When her <u>f</u>riends come over, show them that cool trick you can do with <u>f</u>ish.

14

15

Gg

Every day is a good day to play <u>G</u>iddy-up-Horsey.

Take her to school on the first day, and give her the biggest <u>h</u>ug before you leave.

Feed her <u>i</u>ce cream sundaes for breakfast whenever she wants.

21

Jumping on the bed every night
before bedtime is a must!

Listen to all of her silly <u>K</u>nock-knock jokes.

25

Ll

Make her laugh until she can't take it anymore.

Mm

Sit in the <u>m</u>akeup chair so you can look your best, and hope she doesn't post any pictures online.

29

Nn

Never be late for her weekly <u>n</u>ail appointment because she has to look fabulous.

Oo

Surprise her with a superhero <u>o</u>utfit. You can't be the only hero in the family.

Pp

Always make time for a midday tea party because playdates are so important.

35

Qq

Answer any question she may have,
no matter how tough it may be.

37

Gather all the other super dads and sing all the popular songs from her favorite <u>r</u>adio station.

Ss

Push her as high as you can on the
<u>s</u>wing set at the playground.

Find her the biggest, cutest, and fluffiest <u>T</u>eddy bear on her birthday.

Uu

If she gets all A's on her report card, take her on a magical <u>U</u>nicorn ride.

Vv

Enjoy her <u>v</u>iolin playing; no matter what it sounds like, do your best to keep a smile on your face.

On the <u>w</u>eekend, take her for a shopping spree to her favorite store and buy her whatever she wants.

49

Find the e<u>x</u>tra big bo<u>x</u>es to build the biggest forts.

Never yell at her...no matter how
much trouble she may get into.

53

Zz

Always let her catch some <u>zzz</u>s in your lap because she's your princess...of course.

The End

Tyson Bell is a best-selling children's book author and a veteran teacher. He lives in Columbus, Ohio, where he is a third-grade teacher. He was motivated to write this book to celebrate the powerful relationships between fathers and their daughters.

www.ingramcontent.com/pod-product-compliance
Lightning Source LLC
Chambersburg PA
CBRC090839120626
46551CB00008B/700